ADVENTURES OF A

PIANO TECHNICIAN

by

Donald E. Ellis

www.lskidstuff.com

Adventures of a Piano Technician

ISBN: Softcover 978-1-955581-70-7

Copyright © 2022 by Donald E. Ellis

Adventures of a Piano Technician

QUALIFICATIONS AND LICENSING

In November of 1987 I completed an intense course with the **American School of Piano Tuning** and was awarded a **Certificate of Completion and Diploma** on the 21st day of the month. I Immediately started looking forward to tuning my first piano.

The first tuning after my accreditation and licensing with the State of Virginia was one of my wife's students. I had no confidence in those early days. I returned to two different customer homes to re-tune as I didn't feel satisfied with the work. Once I returned (on the same day) to a West Point nursing home as I felt the repairs were not up to a good standard. Repairs, string replacements, etc. fell naturally into place as I became familiar with the pianos of my customer base.

A business license with the State of Virginia is important. This may be done at the County office. Only once as a piano technician was I asked by a customer if I had a local business license. The gentleman was under the impression that you needed a license in every town in which you worked. I explained that the license covered the State of Virginia.

Business cards may be significant in building a customer base. An example of this is a contract I acquired with Riverside hospital to tune and clean the Grand Piano in their lobby. During the process I would leave a small stack of business cards on the piano to be available as folk stopped by to watch my work. Tuning a piano in the lobby of Costco and placing my business cards there as well is another example of their importance. Business cards are a useful method anytime a technician is tuning in a public place.

In those early days I was working a full-time job and tuning pianos on the evenings and weekends. Scheduled tunings during the week were after 5:00 p.m. with several more on Saturdays. I worked this schedule from 1987 until September 2000 when I retired from the City of Newport News.

I had a delightful career tuning and working on pianos. I wouldn't trade those experiences for anything. I've made many good friends with fond memories.

The mileage on my car attest to the wide area of my customers' base. The areas of coverage included Eastern Shore, Portsmouth, Hampton, Newport News, Suffolk, Smithfield, Williamsburg, Richmond, Hopewell, Gloucester, York County, New Kent County, Deltaville and Matthews County.

AFFILIATIONS

CONTRACTS

WARRANTY TUNINGS

Establishing contracts with colleges and schools are usually acquired through a bid. The lowest bid is chosen in most instances. My contract with the Virginia Commonwealth University Department of Music included a total of forty-two pianos. The contract also included a Baldwin Concert Grand be tuned every Friday morning at 8:30 a.m. This was in preparation for the orchestra to practice.

In September of the new school year at VCU, I tuned pianos twice each week in the department to eventually include all the pianos in the process. As the winter holidays approached it was requested that all pianos be tuned within a seven-day shutdown period at the college. This meant six piano tunings per day. Normally, three pianos a day was a busy schedule for me. I finished all forty-two pianos in the allotted time, but determined never to attempt it again.

I received a call from VCU on a Wednesday afternoon saying they had a concert scheduled in the evening and the pianist who had just flown in from Oklahoma was unhappy with one note on the Baldwin Grand just tuned the previous Friday. Dropping everything, I headed for Richmond.

The pianist was waiting on the stage while people were beginning to arrive for the concert in the auditorium. The pianist pointed to the F above middle C saying that it did not sound right. I began checking the octave for harmonics. After bumping the F a few times I asked him to try it out. He played a few notes and said he was happy with it. I packed up my gear and headed home to Williamsburg.

The Virginia Commonwealth University contract was difficult as I lived fifty miles away. I did not bid the following year.

The school board on the Eastern Shore accepted my bid for the tuning of all school pianos. I would travel to the Eastern Shore every August and tune each of them during this trip. As the tunings would take several days I needed a place to stay. Renting a camper at a campground near the Maryland state line on my first trip, I discovered a trailer was not good. The next year I found a house which had a studio apartment for rent in the central part of Eastern Shore. This apartment became my home base.

It wasn't long before I discovered there was no piano tuner on the Eastern Shore at all. I began receiving calls from teachers at the schools and their friends. Churches too. On this particular Friday I only had two tunings scheduled. The first was about a forty-five minute drive from my house. I would be there at least a couple of hours, voicing the keys before tuning. The next tuning was on the Eastern Shore. It was a church which wanted their piano tuned before a wedding the next day.

I finished the first piano right before noon and headed for the Eastern Shore, arriving at the church about 2:30 in the afternoon. I opened the back door of my car to get my equipment. The back seat was empty. A telephone call confirmed my worst fear. I had left my equipment by the front door of the first customer's house. I had set it by the door and went back to the piano to show the customer the results of the voicing; then, walked out the door and drove to the Eastern Shore.

I promised the church I would return the first thing Saturday morning to make sure the piano was tuned for the wedding. I'm pretty sure I didn't break even financially that day, but did see some great scenery while crossing the Chesapeake Bay Bridge tunnel twice.

Eastern Shore provided other church turnings. Pulling into the parking lot of a new church customer, I did not see any cars parked at the church. Thinking I was a little early, I decided to have a bite of lunch while waiting. Half an hour later no one showed up to let me in. Deciding to try the doors to see if anyone was inside and waiting for me, I walked around the church trying the doors to no avail. All were locked.

About that time the police showed up asking questions. Apparently, I had set off an alarm while trying the doors. While explaining to the officers, a car pulled up demanding to know what was going on. I explained the scheduled tuning for their piano for the service tomorrow. He was very irate saying that he had called no one; and, no one but he could schedule any work for the church. He informed me I was trespassing and that I should leave immediately. I did so. I heard nothing from the church regarding this issue or if their piano was ever tuned.

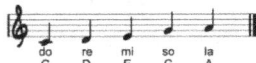

I started spending a whole week on the Eastern Shore tuning as many pianos as I could in one week. Foreseeing this could easily become a two-week project, I ended up giving the contract away to another piano technician. He was a retired minister who lived in Norfolk with his wife. He was unemployed and living off a small Social Security check. Giving him some of my spare equipment and the names of the individuals wanting their pianos tuned, I notified the School Board of the change.

A couple of years later he called thanking me for helping him and also to let me know that he had received a call from a church in North

Carolina wanting him to pastor their church. He seemed very happy about the way things turned out.

I didn't hear again from the School Board of Eastern Shore. By then I had so many customers, I wasn't sure I could handle the contract had they telephoned.

Kimball Console – Vienna

GOOD VIBRATIONS

I was tuning a piano on a Saturday in a church/gymnasium. It was an old Nippon (Yamaha Grand). There were no cars in the parking lot; but, I had keys and let myself in locking the door behind me and doing a quick walk-around to verify that I was the only one there. Then I started tuning the piano.

After about twenty minutes I heard a noise like a drum roll. It was a very clear audible drum roll close by. I did another walk-around to make sure no one else was in the building. Then went back to tuning. About twenty minutes later I heard it again. Getting a little spooked I checked all the rooms once more even checking the parking lot to see if any cars were out there. Nothing!

I went back to the note I had been tuning (a Bb) and as soon as I struck it the drum roll sounded. That was when I noticed there was a drum set on the stage. Every time I played Bb the drum roll sounded. Checking over the drum set I noticed that the small chains underneath the snare drum were touching the bottom of the drum. Switching the lever to take the chains off the snare, I went back to the piano and played the Bb. No drum roll!

Apparently, the vibrations from the Bb caused the snare chains to vibrate. I have since had a few instances where a certain note on the piano would cause something in the room (usually glass) to vibrate.

GODS AND GENERALS

One customer was extremely proud of his piano. He had every right to be. It was a 1849 Chickering Grand in excellent shape. No refurbishing. He just kept it clean and tuned.

Right after tuning this exquisite piano, I was in a piano outlet when the owner of the outlet mentioned he received a call from a Hollywood producer who was looking for a "hundred-year-old grand piano" to be used in a movie then in production called Gods and Generals, a Civil War movie.

I told the outlet owner about my customer having an 1849 Chickering Grand in very good shape. Everyone became excited, especially the owner of the piano itself. I was no longer involved; but heard later that the Hollywood producer turned down the piano. He claimed it was not an authentic Chickering Grand because of the legs.

A Chickering Grand is known for its massive, decorative carvings on the legs. This customer's Grand had small, plain, straight legs. Instead, the producers took an old square grand that was in the back of the piano outlet. For years it had been used as a work table and would produce no sound at all. It was actually sitting on two saw horses.

I went to the movie just to see the piano. The piano was never shown at all; just the back of the lady playing the piano.

The next time I tuned the Chickering Grand the owner showed me an 8x10 glossy photo of a Chickering Grand with straight legs he had printed off the internet.

Chickering Grand – Massive Legs

Chickering Parlor Grand Antique

Massive Legs

1928 Chickering Grand

Small Legs

Chickering Grand – Small Legs

EXPERIENCES

AND

CUSTOMERS

I received a call from a piano teacher who asked if I would tune his piano at no charge in exchange for tuning the pianos for all of his students. I agreed to this on a trial basis. It turned out to be a very good deal as I started getting calls from about twenty people saying their teacher had recommended me.

Soon I was doing Warranty tunings. These were given at no charge to a purchaser of a piano from a piano outlet in the local area. The outlet had two locations. The owner of these piano outlets was also interested in a museum and was accumulating items of interest. They asked if I would be willing to do their warranty tunings. Of course, I said "Yes." The agreement with the two outlets was for a reduced price rather than my usual fee; however, each warranty tuning gave me a new customer.

The areas of coverage for these tunings included Eastern Shore, Portsmouth, Hampton, Newport News, Suffolk, Smithfield, Richmond, Williamsburg, Hopewell, Gloucester, York County, New Kent County, Deltaville and Matthews County.

A gentleman bought a new Yamaha console. He had it delivered and two weeks later I did a free warranty tuning for him. He seemed quite happy with the results. Six months later I called him. The call was a reminder that it was time to tune his piano. His response was "Why? I've already had my piano tuned." Apparently, he was under the impression that a piano only needed one tuning. He told me that if it ever needed tuning again he would call me. I haven't heard from him since. I'm wondering how it sounds?

One Saturday while working in my yard, I received a call from a friend of mine. I had begun to help him get started in the tuning business. He said that he was tuning a piano at a funeral home and had found a broken string on the piano. He was new to repairs and wanted to know if I could replace the string for him. I agreed and headed out to the Petersburg area and the funeral home.

What the friend failed to mention was that a funeral was about to start. The piano was in the same room as the casket which was only about five feet away. Most of the family was sitting on the front row watching me. I can honestly say that I have never replaced a string faster than the one at this funeral home.

Churches were my favorite places for tunings. I always gave churches a discount and never charged for a tuning at a church I was attending. The least favorite place to tune is in hotels. Their pianos seemed to be abused. Drinks are spilled. Pianos are moved from place to place and not stored properly.

In all the years I have tuned pianos I can honestly say that I had a very good relationship with my customers. My customers trusted me and considered me a good friend. If they were not going to be at home during the tuning, they would leave the door unlocked with a check on the piano. I even had a maid give me a blank check after the tuning. I made sure she filled it out herself rather than me leaving with a blank check. In all the years of tuning pianos I can only remember four times I did not get paid.

An interesting experience occurred regarding a customer defrauded by another piano tuner. A lady bought a used piano from the piano outlet where I had a contract to do all their warranty tunings. Anyone buying a piano from the outlet would get their first tuning free. Warranty tunings are usually scheduled two weeks after the purchase. This gives the piano time to settle in its new location. I would get a card from the piano outlet with the name, address, the telephone number of the purchaser, and the type of piano they bought. I would usually wait about two weeks after delivery before calling and making an appointment.

Apparently, the lady didn't understand the process and immediately looked up piano technicians in the telephone book and said that she was ready for her piano tuning.

The technician came out and told her that the piano needed a little work before tuning. He removed the action of her piano saying that he would work on it from his shop. He asked for a check for $250 to cover expenses. If it came to more than that amount he would collect it when he brought the action back.

After he left the lady became upset. She was not aware the piano needed work when she bought it. She called the piano outlet to complain. The manager said that there was nothing wrong with the piano and the technician who came to her house wasn't authorized to do their warranty work. She immediately called the tuner demanding her check and the piano action be brought back to her house.

When I came to her house to tune her piano the action was sitting on the floor by the piano. I looked it over carefully before re-installing it. I could find nothing wrong with the action. After tuning her newly purchased used piano, she was happy.

A tuning I will always remember took place in York County on September 11, 2001. I was about halfway finished when the lady called me to come into the den to see the news. I stared at the TV for several minutes before I realized what I was watching. The first plane had already hit the towers; but, as I was watching the second plane hit. I couldn't believe this was actually happening; it was like I was dreaming.

To be honest, I do not remember finishing the tuning, although I am sure I did. Everything was a blur. My brain was still trying to process what had actually happened. I will never forget that moment.

In the auditorium of a Catholic High School is the remembrance of a tuning which did not go well. No one was happy with the tuning. I was well into the tuning when it started raining very hard outside where the cheerleaders were practicing. They decided to move into the auditorium and continue practicing.

Of course, normal practice for cheerleaders is to see how loud you can yell, and even though they were at the other end of the auditorium, the sound carried quite well. I absolutely could not hear the notes on the piano and they had no other place to practice.

I tried my best to finish the tuning, but was very unhappy with the way it sounded. I tried explaining the situation to the person who contacted me to tune the piano, but am not sure he was very understanding. Obviously, I never heard from them again.

A good friend of mine was getting married in her home in about thirty days. She called me saying that the vocalist tried to practice with the piano; but could not as the instrument was so far off pitch. They wanted to know if I could tune it to standard pitch in time for the ceremony.

It took four tunings to get the piano up to standard pitch, plus one more time just before the ceremony. The wedding went off very well and they are still happily married.

Fischer Victorian Upright

DISTINCTIVE
PIANOS

I imagine most piano technicians have a favorite make of piano they enjoy tuning and working on. When I first started this, my second career, a technician friend told me that if he could afford it, he would advertise that he would only tune Yamaha pianos. I agree they are one of the easiest pianos to tune and they do hold their tuning; but, I also love to tune older Baldwin pianos. Their sound seems to mellow with age.

As far as working on individual pianos, Spinets are very difficult to work on; but, the one piano most technicians refuse to tune is a piano that has a "bird cage action." They seem to be a design found mostly in pianos from Great Britain.

The technical name for this type of action is an "over-damper system." The term "bird cage" is used because the damper wires are in front of the hammers and give the impression of vertical bars like a cage.

My experience with birdcage action pianos (three times) required removing the piano action in order to place the mutes on the strings; however, with the action removed you cannot play any notes. You can only pluck the strings with your fingers or possibly some kind of a pick. This will take three times longer to tune. The technician will not be able to play any chords. One really cannot tell if the piano is harmonic.

My first encounter with a birdcage piano was for a good friend who asked me as a favor to tune the piano because he was trying to sell it and wanted it to sound good. I agreed; but told him afterward that I never wanted to see a birdcage again. I was able to pluck octaves to check the tuning; however, it took me three hours to finish not to mention the blisters on my fingers from plucking the strings.

Possibly a year later, I received a call from a lady who told me that a friend of mine had recommended me to tune her piano. She didn't mention the friend's name; however, when I saw the piano I immediately knew who the good friend was. It was the same birdcage piano that I had tuned for him months before.

Several years later I received a call from a lady in the county of New Kent wanting her piano tuned. Arriving I immediately spotted the piano, a birdcage. At first I told her that I don't tune this type of piano and explained the difficulties involved in tuning a birdcage piano. She pleaded with me to tune it at any price. I quoted a price quite a bit over my regular fee and mentioned that I would come back the next day and bring my daughter. My daughter had become my partner sharing the workload. She joined me in tuning this piano. Each us taking turns plucking the strings.

The lady agreed and we both came the next day. It still took us three hours and my daughter informed me to never again ask her to tune a birdcage piano. I agreed. This was the last time I saw a birdcage action piano.

Vintage Bird Cage

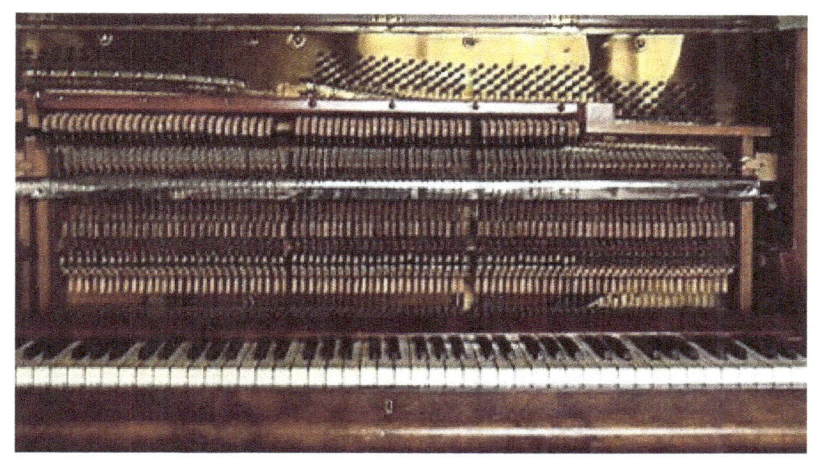

Waldmann, Berlin Birdcage

Player Pianos

There are many varieties of player pianos. Older models were once purchased with the selected music hole-punched determining the notes to be played. The purchase of fully intact antique player pianos is rare as the music has aged and become fragile. Newer models contain digital equipment to produce the sound. These older models are now purchased simply as a lovely piece of antique furniture without the paper rolls once used for music.

An interesting experience concerning a player piano occurred when a customer called me to tune her piano telling me that I needed to be there on a specific day and time. The reason? She had a player piano technican coming from Maryland to remove the player action before the tuning.

I had tuned player pianos before; but, they were older models with easy access to strings and pins. This piano was a newer model and a bit more complicated. The tech arrived that morning and removed the player action. All was ready when I arrived and began tuning the piano.

When the tuning was completed, the technician from Maryland began putting the player parts back into the piano. To do all this the customer had to pay the technician's gas, along with one night in a motel plus my tuning fee. The customer seemed happy; yet, it did seem a bit expensive.

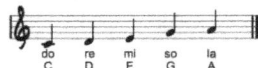

Pianola

Sterling Library Mission Style

Old West

Wurlitzer

Gulbransen Mahogany Player Piano

Schafer & Sons Player Piano

Becker Bros. Upright Player Piano

1911 Melville Clark "Apollo"

Antique Player Piano

NURSING HOMES
AND
THE ELDERLY

I had numerous tunings for nursing homes which were always interesting. Once as I was setting my equipment up to begin, I noticed that the residents were coming into the room finding seats at the tables. It was time for Bingo!

I tried to ignore the noise. Soon an elderly lady close to me looked over and asked if I could please keep it down so she could hear the caller. The piano was tuned after bingo.

A resident residing at a similar nursing home was an older gentleman who pulled up a chair beside me to watch. After finishing he asked if he could try it out. He was quite the accomplished pianist. He explained me that he was the one who kept bugging the staff about getting the piano tuned.

A piano technician will encounter many interesting times with elderly customers. Once in early spring I arrived at an appointment to find an elderly lady at the door in a thick robe with fuzzy slippers. The house was extremely warm. The thermostat must have been set on 80 degrees. Fortunately, I didn't fall asleep during the tuning, but I did come very close.

Another elderly client's piano was approximately a half-step flat. I took my time bringing the entire piano up to the A-440 (standard pitch). Finishing, I let her try it out to see how it sounded. Immediately, she said that she didn't like it. The sound was too bright.

I explained to her that it was tuned higher in order to bring it up to standard pitch. She was very unhappy and asked me to please take it back down to where it was before I started tuning. I spent the next forty-five minutes tuning the piano back down to a half-step lower to standard pitch. She was happily playing her piano when I left.

Then there was the elderly gentleman who insisted that his piano be tuned to European pitch. Fortunately, my electronic tuner had a setting for European pitch and I used it to tune his piano. He claimed that it was the only pitch for Classical music.

GLORIOUS

PIANOS

A unique piano design.

Hamburg Model A

Steinway

Exotic Burl Wood

Rococo

1950 Steinway B

Lindeblad

Hallet & Davis Square Grand

Early Chickering Square Grand

Steinway & Sons

Cottage Upright

An exhibition of

World's Oldest Piano

Tomkison, Thomas

Grand Piano

Circa 1815